HUMPTY DUMPTY

HUMPTY DUMPTY

As told by **Kin Eagle**

illustrated by **Rob Gilbert**

Gareth Stevens Publishing
A WORLD ALMANAC EDUCATION GROUP COMPANY

For a free color catalog describing Gareth Stevens'
list of high-quality books and multimedia programs,
call 1-800-542-2595 (USA) or 1-800-461-9120 (Canada).
Gareth Stevens Publishing's Fax: (414) 225-0377.

Library of Congress Cataloging-in-Publication Data available
upon request from publisher. Fax (414) 225-0377 for the
attention of the Publishing Records Department.

ISBN 0-8368-2667-1

This edition first published in 2000 by
Gareth Stevens Publishing
A World Almanac Education Group Company
1555 North RiverCenter Drive, Suite 201
Milwaukee, WI 53212 USA

Text © 1999 by Kin Eagle. Illustrations © 1999 by Rob Gilbert.
Music © 1999 by Daniel Adlerman. Original edition published
by Charlesbridge Publishing, 85 Main Street, Watertown, MA 02472.

All rights to this edition reserved to Gareth Stevens, Inc. No part of this
book may be reproduced, stored in a retrieval system, or transmitted in any
form or by any means, electronic, mechanical, photocopying, recording, or
otherwise without the prior written permission of the publisher except for
the inclusion of brief quotations in an acknowledged review.

Printed in the United States of America

1 2 3 4 5 6 7 8 9 04 03 02 01 00

*For Mom—
a truly good egg!*
—K.E.

*For Sky—
love, Papa*
—R.G.

Humpty Dumpty sat on a wall,
Humpty Dumpty had a great fall.

All the king's horses and all the king's men
Couldn't put Humpty together again.

Humpty Dumpty hiked up the hill,
Humpty Dumpty took a big spill.

All of the children outside at play
Ran as fast as they could to get out of his way.

Humpty Dumpty fell down a well,
Humpty Dumpty cracked his great shell.

All the queen's sons and even her daughter
Couldn't lift Humpty from out of the water.

Humpty Dumpty sailed on a boat,
Humpty Dumpty splashed in the moat.
All of the gators and all of the crocs
Were dreaming of Humpty with bagel and lox!

Humpty Dumpty walked down the road,
Humpty Dumpty tripped on a toad.

All of the jesters with all of their jokes
Tried hard to keep Humpty from spilling his yolk.

Humpty Dumpty jumped into the lake,
Humpty Dumpty started to break.

Rushing to save him, all of the knights
Had rusted steel armor and water-logged tights!

Humpty Dumpty rode a white horse,
Humpty Dumpty was thrown with such force

All of the shepherds and all of the sheep
Were woken quite startled from out of their sleep.

Humpty Dumpty climbed onto my lap,
Humpty Dumpty curled up for a nap.

When we are together, we're safe as can be,
Because I love Humpty and Humpty loves me!

HUMPTY DUMPTY

Music by Daniel Adlerman

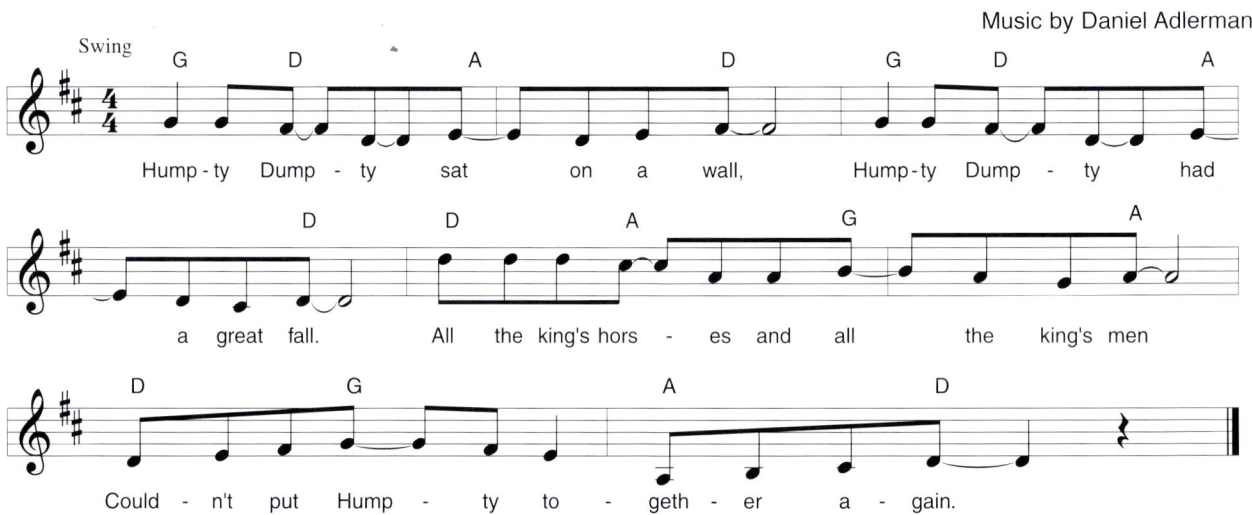

Hump-ty Dump-ty sat on a wall, Hump-ty Dump-ty had a great fall. All the king's hors-es and all the king's men Could-n't put Hump-ty to-geth-er a-gain.

2. Humpty Dumpty hiked up the hill,
   Humpty Dumpty took a big spill.
   All of the children outside at play
   Ran as fast as they could to get out of his way.

3. Humpty Dumpty fell down a well,
   Humpty Dumpty cracked his great shell.
   All the queen's sons and even her daughter
   Couldn't lift Humpty from out of the water.

4. Humpty Dumpty sailed on a boat,
   Humpty Dumpty splashed in the moat.
   All of the gators and all of the crocs
   Were dreaming of Humpty with bagel and lox!

5. Humpty Dumpty walked down the road,
   Humpty Dumpty tripped on a toad.
   All of the jesters with all of their jokes
   Tried hard to keep Humpty from spilling his yolk.

6. Humpty Dumpty jumped into the lake,
   Humpty Dumpty started to break.
   Rushing to save him, all of the knights
   Had rusted steel armor and water-logged tights!

7. Humpty Dumpty rode a white horse,
   Humpty Dumpty was thrown with such force
   All of the shepherds and all of the sheep
   Were woken quite startled from out of their sleep.

8. Humpty Dumpty climbed onto my lap,
   Humpty Dumpty curled up for a nap.
   When we are together, we're safe as can be,
   Because I love Humpty and Humpty loves me!